Hi!

Welcome to your Coffee Self-Talk™ Journal. I made this blank journal available so you could have a companion to go with your copy of the book, Coffee Self-Talk.

Fill this journal with your own Coffee Self-Talk scripts, glowing affirmations, and juicy reminders to live your most magical life. Fill it with luscious love notes to yourself, color in it, draw hearts and stars and rainbows everywhere, if you like. Use it to journal all the ideas rolling around in your head, making lists of ways to live your best life, business ideas, story ideas, travel ideas, dreams, goals... you name it. Fill it with everything YOU!

You are worthy.
You are amazing.
You are love.

All my very best to you, and may every day be amazing!

Kristen

Kristen Helmstetter
Author, Coffee Self-Talk

Come join us! facebook.com/groups/coffeeselftalk